Francisco Coronado

Francisco Coronado

Don Nardo

Franklin Watts
A Division of Scholastic Inc.
New York • Toronto • London • Auckland • Sydney
Mexico City • New Delhi • Hong Kong
Danbury, Connecticut

Note to readers: Definitions for words in **bold** can be found in the Glossary at the back of this book.

Photographs ©: Art Resource, NY: 13 (Scala), 19 (Schalkwijk); Corbis-Bettmann: 38 (Kevin Fleming), 26, 27, 32, 37; Michael Snell/Shade of the Cottonwood, L.L.C.: 43; North Wind Picture Archives: 41 (N. Carter), 9, 21, 22, 31, 34, 35, 44, 51; National Park Service: 14 (painting by Nevin Kempthorne, photograph by Dave Bly); Peter Arnold Inc./Kim Heacox: 50; Stock Montage, Inc.: 5 bottom, 24; Superstock, Inc.: 47 (A.K.G, Berlin/Castillo de Chapultepec, Mexico), 30 (David David Gallery, Philadelphia), 25 (Ronald Thomas), 2, 33; Terry Donnelly: 39; The Art Archive: 11 (Eileen Tweedy/Private Collection), 18 (Dagli Orti/Galleria degli Uffizi, Florence); The Image Works/Stuart Cohen: 16; Tom Bean: 42.

Cover illustration, 5 top, 49 by Stephen Marchesi.

Map by XNR Productions, Inc.

The illustration on the cover shows the Spanish explorer Francisco Vásquez de Coronado. The photograph opposite the title page shows Canyon de Chelly in Arizona.

Library of Congress Cataloging-in-Publication Data

Nardo, Don, 1947–
    Francisco Coronado / Don Nardo
        p.cm.— (Watts Library)
        Includes bibliographical references (p.) and index.
        ISBN 0-531-11974-2 (lib. bdg.)   0-531-16576-0 (pbk.)
    1. Coronado, Francisco Vásquez de, 1510–1554—Juvenile literature. 2. Explorers—America—Biography—Juvenile literature. 3. Explorers—Spain—Biography—Juvenile literature. 4. Southwest, New—Discovery and exploration—Spanish—Juvenile literature. 5. America—Discovery and exploration—Spanish—Juvenile literature. 6. Indians of North America—First contact with Europeans—Southwest, New—Juvenile literature. [1. Coronado, Francisco Vásquez de, 1510–1554. 2. Explorers. 3. Southwest, New—Discovery and exploration. 4. America—Discovery and exploration—Spanish.] I. Title. II. Series.
E125. V3 N37   2001
979'.01'092—dc2
[B]
                                                                                                00-049986

Contents

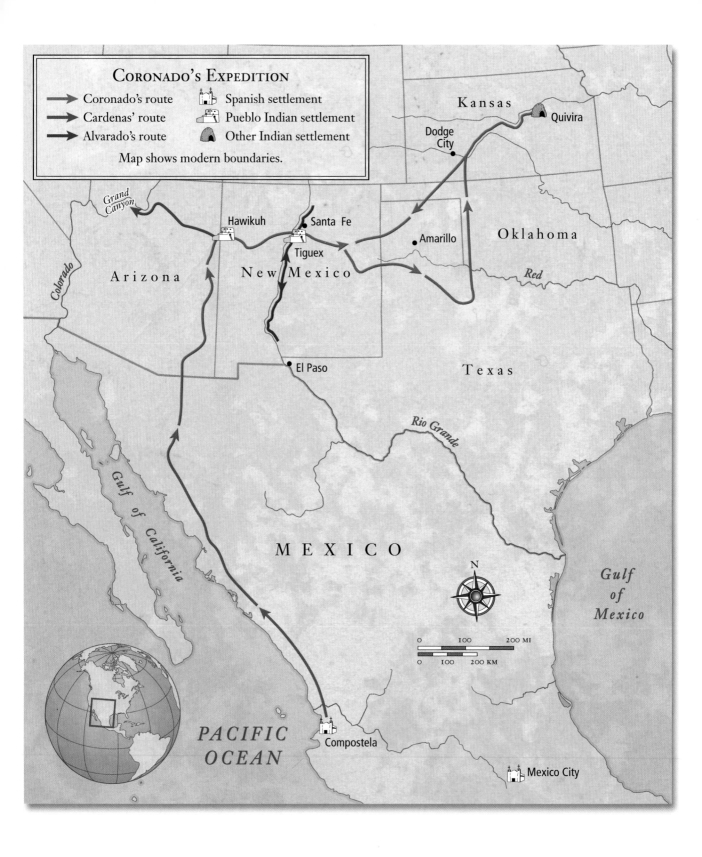

CORONADO'S EXPEDITION

→ Coronado's route
→ Cardenas' route
→ Alvarado's route

🏛 Spanish settlement
🏚 Pueblo Indian settlement
⛺ Other Indian settlement

Map shows modern boundaries.

Kansas

Quivira

Dodge City

Oklahoma

Grand Canyon

Hawikuh

Santa Fe

Tiguex

Amarillo

Colorado

Arizona

New Mexico

Red

El Paso

Texas

Rio Grande

MEXICO

Gulf of California

N

Gulf of Mexico

0   100   200 MI
0   100   200 KM

PACIFIC OCEAN

Compostela

Mexico City

Chapter One

The Fabled Seven Cities

The Spanish explorer Francisco Vásquez de Coronado wanted to find the legendary Seven Cities of Cíbola. Like other people in his day, he had heard that these cities lay somewhere in the unexplored lands north of Mexico. Supposedly, they were large, rich, splendid places with wide streets and many-storied buildings, some of them having domes and decorations of solid gold.

By the time of Coronado's birth, around 1510, stories about these cities and their fabulous treasures were already very old. Roughly 750 years earlier, the story said that armies of Moors swept out of northern Africa and crossed the Strait of Gibraltar, at the western end of the Mediterranean Sea. The Moors, who were **Muslims**, followers of the religion known as Islam, overran most of what is now Spain and Portugal. Because the original inhabitants of the region were Christians, they strongly objected to the Moorish conquest, and over the years many Christians tried to escape.

The legend of the Seven Cities stems from one group of escaping Christians who took a fateful journey in about A.D. 1000, roughly one thousand years ago. According to the story, seven Christian bishops and their followers first built some **stout** ships. Then they set sail westward into the vast reaches of the then mysterious sea that we know today as the Atlantic Ocean. In time, these **wayfarers** supposedly reached a new land on the far side of the sea. And there, each bishop directed the building of a great city, so that there were seven cities in all, each filled with gold and other valuables.

Discovering a New World

The legend of the Seven Cities and their wonderful treasures persisted for centuries. Many people wanted to go looking for these fabled places. But for a long time, no one dared to strike out over the great sea, mainly because they were not sure that there was really land on the other side. Some, believing that the world was flat, feared that they might fall off the end of the

earth. Others worried that those old sailors' tales of terrifying sea monsters that could swallow a person in a single bite might be true.

By the early 1500s, when Coronado was a boy in Spain, these fears had disappeared. The renowned Italian explorer Christopher Columbus had shown in 1492 that there were indeed habitable lands on the other side of the Atlantic Ocean. Sailing for the Spanish queen, Isabella, Columbus had made several voyages and discovered islands—the West Indies in the Caribbean Sea—filled with lush vegetation and inhabited by native peoples living in simple villages.

Many sailors believed that the waters of the Atlantic Ocean were filled with scary sea monsters.

It was clear to the first European explorers that these islands did not contain the legendary Seven Cities. But they soon learned that an entire continent larger than Europe lay beyond. They hoped that this unknown territory would be the land where the Spanish bishops of old had established their treasure cities.

It was not long before all of Mexico, which at the time was appropriately known as New Spain, came under the control of the Spanish. They explored its valleys and plains, established new towns and farms, and forced many of the American Indians to become their servants. In addition, a good many Spanish searched high and low for any gold or other natural riches the region might harbor. However, it rapidly became clear that the fabled Seven Cities were not located in this newly conquered land.

Rich Indians in the North?

The Spanish decided to search for the Seven Cities in the unexplored territories stretching north of New Spain. They had no idea that this region was many times larger than New Spain and that someday it would be divided into two huge and

CONQVISTA DE MEXICO POR CORTES. AÇ7

The Spanish in Mexico

Between 1519 and 1521, the Spanish soldier and adventurer Hernando Cortés conquered most of what is now Mexico. The Aztecs and other American Indians in the area tried to fight off the invaders, but they lost their battles with the Spanish. They lost mainly because the Spanish possessed gunpowder, cannon, armor, and other advanced weapons. From that time, until Mexico became independent of Spain in 1821, the Spanish controlled the area.

prosperous countries—the United States and Canada. And because almost all of this area was uncharted wilderness, it was easy to get lost or suffer other hardships in it. Explorers might die of thirst or starvation. Or they might be attacked by wild animals or unknown tribes of savages. The first major expedition launched to find the Seven Cities did, in fact, get lost.

About three hundred men led by a Spaniard named Pánfilo de Narváez set out in 1528 into what is now the southern United States and simply disappeared.

Many years later, four survivors of the Narváez expedition staggered into New Spain. One of these men, Álvar Núñez Cabeza de Vaca, was asked to report to the **viceroy** (a kind of governor) in the capital, Mexico City. The viceroy, Don Antonio de Mendoza, asked Cabeza de Vaca what had happened to Narváez and the other members of the expedition. They had all died, Cabeza de Vaca claimed, during a difficult trek through seemingly endless insect-infested jungles, steep mountain ranges, and desert wastelands. "No other [people have ever] encountered such great dangers," Cabeza de Vaca later wrote, "or had such a miserable and disastrous outcome."

Then Mendoza anxiously asked about the Seven Cities. Had the explorers found them and gazed on their fabled treasures? Cabeza de Vaca told Mendoza the disappointing news—the members of the expedition had seen no cities, no gold, and no other places or items of any significant value. Yet Cabeza de Vaca still had a glimmer of hope. He spoke with a group of American Indians living in a valley in the region that would later be called Arizona who told him that they sometimes traded with another group of Indians who lived far to the north. The members of that faraway tribe, they claimed, lived in cities featuring large huts containing jewels and other precious materials.

Neither Cabeza de Vaca nor Mendoza could say for sure whether the Arizona Indians were telling the truth about their rich trading partners. But the viceroy felt that it was worth a try to send a small scouting party to investigate. He sent a **friar** named Marcos de Niza, who left New Spain with a few men in February 1539. Friar Marcos returned in August of that same year. He claimed that he had heard many stories from

Francisco Vásquez de Coronado was selected to lead the latest search for the Seven Cities.

Another Treasure Hunter

Hernando de Soto, a Spanish explorer, began his own search for gold around the same time as Friar Marcos. Like several other European explorers, De Soto wanted to find the fabled Seven Cities, but his main goal was to acquire treasure no matter where he found it. He landed in what is now known as Florida in May 1539. He traveled toward the east and eventually became the first European to see the Mississippi River.

American Indians about cities lying farther north and about Indians who owned and traded gold and other valuables.

To Mendoza, the report given by Friar Marcos seemed strong enough evidence to mount a full-scale expedition to seek the Seven Cities. The viceroy knew that he would need a man of exceptional abilities and character to lead such an important enterprise. He could think of no one more qualified than one of New Spain's leading citizens—Francisco Vásquez de Coronado.

This photograph shows the city of Salamanca, Spain, near where Coronado lived in his youth.

Chapter Two

The Adventure Begins

Born in 1510, Francisco Vásquez de Coronado grew up in a large, comfortable family home outside of the Spanish university town of Salamanca. If he had been his father's first-born son, he would have inherited the family fortune, the traditional custom at the time. In that case, he would likely have taken charge of the family estate in Spain and never

King Charles V of Spain

have traveled to New Spain and become an explorer. He would have raised horses and other animals, managed a large staff of farmhands and servants, and perhaps spent many a pleasant evening on his front porch listening to guitar music. Since Coronado was not his family's first-born son, he had to find some other way of obtaining property and making a name for himself.

In those days, the most promising way of gaining fame and fortune was to leave Spain and seek adventure and gold in the newfound lands across the sea. So Coronado decided that he must find some way to obtain a position in New Spain. When he was twenty-four, he heard that one of his friends from Salamanca, Don Antonio de Mendoza, had been appointed viceroy of New Spain. Mendoza agreed to take Coronado with him. In 1535 they sailed together for New Spain, eager to serve their king, Charles V, as well as to gain personal success and wealth.

Gaining Wealth and Influence

After reaching New Spain, Coronado did everything he could to increase his social position and influence. Through Mendoza, for instance, he obtained a seat on the council that

Mexico's New and Growing Capital

When Coronado first arrived in Mexico, he lived in the rapidly growing capital—Mexico City. Only a few years before, in 1521, the Spanish had begun to transform the older Aztec Indian city of Tenochtitlan, which had been captured by Hernando Cortés, into a European-style town. They erected a new main plaza and laid out new streets in a regular grid pattern, with square lots for houses and several pleasant wooded parks placed among them at intervals. (The native Aztecs were forced to live in crude huts in a separate quarter in the northern part of the city.)

governed the colonial capital, Mexico City. In 1537, Coronado married Beatriz de Estrada, the daughter of Alonso de Estrada, a former royal treasurer of New Spain. Beatriz's father, who was by now deceased, had been one of the wealthiest men in the colony.

Coronado also showed Mendoza that he was a capable military leader. The viceroy was alarmed when a group of slaves working at a local silver mine rebelled, killed some guards, and elected a "king." Mendoza gave Coronado command of a company of soldiers and asked him put down the rebellion. With his troops, Coronado quickly stopped the rebellion. Coronado's swift victory impressed the viceroy so much that he made his friend governor of the province of New Galicia, which was located northwest of Mexico City.

Coronado was quick to take advantage of this new position. We know this thanks to a local Spaniard named Pedro de Castañeda, who later wrote a chronicle of the first few years of Coronado's explorations. According to Castañeda, "at the time [Coronado] was appointed governor, he was traveling through New Spain as an official inspector, and in this way he gained the friendship of many worthy men who afterward went on his expedition with him."

Coronado Assembles an Expedition

Soon after Coronado became governor of New Galicia, Mendoza decided it was time to mount an expedition to search for the fabled Seven Cities of Gold. The viceroy appointed Coronado leader of the venture. Mendoza did this, Castañeda wrote, "because he considered him to be wise, skillful, and intelligent, besides being a gentleman."

After much preparation, Coronado assembled his expedition in Compostela, the capital of New Galicia, in February

This illustration shows what members of Coronado's cavalry may have worn.

1540. Mendoza and many other Spanish nobles were there to witness what Castañeda called "the most brilliant company ever collected in the Indies [the Americas] to go in search of new lands." This company included some three hundred military troops. About 240 of them were **cavalry**, or horse soldiers, and the other 60 were foot soldiers. Most of the men wore heavy metal breastplates and helmets, and for weapons they carried crossbows and primitive guns called **arquebuses**.

The expedition also included about eight hundred American Indians, who carried bows and spears. A few hundred additional Indians, along with some African slaves, were included to do the camp chores and look after the animals.

Once everyone was assembled, a priest conducted a **mass**, a Catholic religious ceremony, to bless them and their mission into the unknown. Then, as told in Castañeda's account, Mendoza "made them a very eloquent short speech, telling

The Arquebus

The Spanish and French developed the arquebus, the first portable gun, in the early sixteenth century. The arquebus worked by pulling a trigger, which brought a flaming match into contact with a small pan of gunpowder. The powder ignited, creating an explosion that discharged a small ball-shaped bullet.

them of the **fidelity** [loyalty] they owed to their general and showing them clearly the benefits which this expedition might afford." The first benefit, according to the viceroy, was that the Spaniards would be able to convert many native peoples to Christianity. Second, the expedition would likely find gold, jewels, and other valuable treasures, making its members rich beyond their dreams. And finally, they would add new territory to Spain's growing empire and thereby gain the favor of the king.

A Slow and Difficult Journey

The next day, Monday, February 23, 1540, "the army started off with its colors flying," according to Castañeda. At first, everyone was excited as they headed northward toward the mysterious region they called Cíbola, which is now the southern United States. But their attitude changed when the journey proved slow and difficult and they began to run out of food. "Although we took all possible care of the small supply

Many Animals Killed on the Rocks

In a letter to the viceroy, Coronado reported that Friar Marcos's account of Cíbola was inaccurate: "Everything which the friar had said was found to be quite the reverse . . . . He said that the way would be plain and good, and that there would be only one small hill . . . . And the truth is, that there are mountains . . . [that] could not be crossed without there being great danger of the horses falling over them. And it was so bad that a large number of animals . . . were lost . . . on account of the roughness of the rocks."

The spirits of members of the expedition seemed dim as they struggled over rough terrain and faced diminishing food supplies.

of provisions which we carried, it gave out," Coronado wrote to Mendoza on August 3, 1540. "And this is not to be wondered at, because the road is rough and long." Coronado wanted to make better time. So in April, he took a small force of eighty horsemen and a few foot soldiers and pushed on, ordering the main part of the army to follow at its own pace.

Eventually, Coronado and his men reached what is now known as southern Arizona. Friar Marcos, who had scouted the region for Mendoza the year before, had claimed that there was a city of several thousand people here—Chichilticali. But Coronado was bitterly disappointed to find only a single, broken-down mud hut on the site. Still, he held out hope that the legendary golden cities lay somewhere beyond. Moving on, he led his men into what is now northern New Mexico. On the night of July 6, 1540, the company approached Hawikuh, which Friar Marcos had claimed was the first of the Seven Cities. They camped in a meadow, unable to see the city, which lay beyond some nearby low hills. It is likely that few of the Spaniards slept well that night, for they believed that soon they would all be very rich and famous men.

Coronado and his party faced more disappointment when they reached what we know as southern Arizona.

Instead of finding golden buildings and untold riches, Coronado had stumbled upon the pueblos of the Zuni Indians.

Chapter Three

Into Zuni Territory

On the morning of July 7, 1540, Coronado and his men broke camp and eagerly made their way to the top of the nearest hill. From there, they hoped to feast their eyes on the first of the fabulous golden cities of Cíbola. Instead of what they expected—a vast city with wide streets and towers of marble and gold—they saw a small cluster of huts made of dried mud. The huts were square-shaped, drab and colorless, and also featureless, except for a few small window openings in some of the walls. Pedro de Castañeda, who witnessed the scene firsthand, later called it "a little, crowded village, looking as if it had been crumpled all up together. There are ranch houses in New Spain which make a better appearance at a distance."

Coronado and his men were surprised, disappointed, and angry. According to Castañeda: "When [we] saw the first village [of] Cíbola, such were the curses that some hurled at Friar Marcos that I pray God may protect him from [my comrades]." Indeed, it was clear that the friar had been either mistaken or lying when he said there was a golden city here. The Spaniards were unaware that what they had found was instead Hawikuh, one of the major settlements of the Zuni Indians.

The Battle of Hawikuh

From the hilltop, the Spaniards could see that a long line of native warriors had gathered in front of the village. These fierce-looking warriors had long hair and were armed with bows and arrows and knives. They had spread cornmeal on the ground, creating a line that they obviously did not want the strangers to cross.

Coronado wanted to avoid a battle, for his men were hungry and weary from their long trek. "I sent the army-master, Don Garcia Lopez, Friar Daniel, and Friar Luis," he later wrote, to tell the native peoples "that we were not coming to do them any harm . . . . But they, being a proud people, were little affected, because it seemed to them that we were few in number, and that they would not have any difficulty in conquering us." The defiant Zuni fired arrows at the peace party, which in turn quickly retreated. In this attack, Friar Luis's robe was pierced by an arrow, but luckily he was not wounded.

Seeing that there was no choice left but to counter-attack, Coronado ordered his soldiers to form ranks and charge. Seeing these armored soldiers rushing at them, the Zunis suddenly took flight, most of them toward the village. The Spaniards followed, advancing on Hawikuh. "That was where the food was," Coronado remembered, "of which we stood in such great need . . . . The hunger which we suffered would not permit of any delay."

Reaching the town, the Spaniards attacked one of its defensive walls. But for a while, they could make little headway, mainly because the defenders kept raining arrows and large stones down on them. "For myself," said Coronado, "they knocked me down to the ground twice with countless great stones . . . and if I had not been protected by the very good headpiece [helmet] which I wore, I think that the outcome would have been bad for me." Luckily for Coronado, he was also protected by Don Garcia Lopez de Cardenas, the man who had led the failed peace party. Don Garcia covered the general's body with his own and then pulled Coronado away from the deadly spray of arrows and rocks.

Though they had gotten off to a slow start in their assault, Coronado and his soldiers had the advantage of their metal armor and superior weapons. So eventually, they managed to

Fearing their village would be destroyed and their people killed, the Zunis surrendered.

fight their way into the town. Perhaps fearing that their women and children would be **massacred**, the Zuni warriors quickly surrendered. After their victory, the Spaniards relieved their hunger by eating their fill of the village corn supply.

Skilled, Hardworking Farmers

After taking the Zuni village by force, Coronado decided that it was time for his troops to re-group. He waited for the main body of the army to catch up and join him at Hawikuh. Then he divided his men into small raiding parties and sent them out to capture other Zuni villages in the surrounding territory, a task which proved fairly quick and easy. In all, there were seven towns, each inhabited by a few poor Zunis. They were clearly not the legendary Seven Cities.

However, Coronado and his men soon learned that these Zunis, though poor, were skilled and hardworking farmers who grew **maize**, a kind of corn. The Zunis ground up the maize to make flat cakes that the Spaniards came to call tortillas. "They make the best corn cakes I have ever seen anywhere," Coronado wrote. In addition, they "have very good salt in crystals, which they bring from a lake a day's journey distant from here." The Zunis also used clay to craft fine pottery bowls and jars, on which they painted religious and other images.

As for the Zunis' houses, Coronado reckoned that there

Coronado and his expedition were impressed by the Zunis' skills as farmers.

Maize

Unlike the yellow, sweet corn familiar to most people today, maize has hard, many-colored kernels. Maize grows well in the hot, dry climate of the American southwest, homeland of the Zunis.

were about two hundred of them in Hawikuh. One of his men later described them this way:

"They have two and three and four and five stories. The walls are about a handbreadth thick; the sticks of timber [used for bracing] are as large as the wrist . . . . The walls are of dirt and mud, [and] the doors of the houses are like the hatchways of ships. The houses are close together, each joined to the others."

Such tightly packed clusters of dried mud houses soon came to be called **pueblos**, from the Spanish word for "villages."

What the Zunis Wore

In a letter written in 1541, an unknown member of Coronado's band described the Zunis' clothing. "Some of these people," he began, "wear cloaks of cotton . . . and of tanned deer skin, and they wear shoes made of these skins, reaching up to the knees. They also make cloaks of the skins of hares and rabbits . . . . The women wear cloaks . . . reaching down to their feet, with girdles."

An Explorer in His Heart

From conversations with the Zunis, Coronado learned that there were other towns lying far to the northwest and the northeast. In these places, there were supposedly "better houses than those of the natives of this country," and the inhabitants were ruled by lords "who were served with dishes of gold." Coronado was unsure if he should believe these stories. He suspected that the Zunis might just be telling him this so that he and his army

would go away. But he decided that it would be worthwhile to explore more of this vast, uncharted territory. In the long run, he reasoned, Spain would surely benefit, for it might be able to claim and eventually inhabit much of it. In his heart and mind, Coronado was becoming less of a treasure hunter and more of true explorer.

The Zunis encouraged Coronado's expedition to continue their search by saying that there were wealthy cities to the north.

Coronado dreamed of discovering what was beyond the desolate plains near the Zunis.

Chapter Four

Beyond the Horizon

In late July 1540, Coronado and his army still occupied the Zuni town of Hawikuh, which they called Granada. Coronado was eager to find out what lands, peoples, and possible treasures might lie beyond the horizon to the north, west, and east. He hoped that the largely flat, sandy, arid plain in which Hawikuh was situated would give way to lush, forested hillsides dotted with sparkling streams and wealthy towns ripe for the picking. But for the moment, the injuries he had sustained in the battle of Hawikuh made him too weak to travel. He had to spend most of his time lying or sitting quietly in a comfortable makeshift bed his men had made for him in one of the Zuni huts. So while his wounds were healing, he decided to send out some small exploratory parties, each of them commanded by one of his most trusted officers.

Land of the Hopis

The Zuni claimed that there were seven larger settlements many miles to the west, in the region they called Tuzan. Could these be the fabled Seven Cities of Cíbola, many of the Spaniards wondered? Coronado selected a party of twenty men and put them under the command of one of his officers, Don Pedro de Tobar. Guided by one of the Zunis, this group headed west for some 75 miles (120 kilometers). And sure enough, the group found a number of settlements in the land of Tuzan.

Once more, however, the Spaniards were disappointed, for these were mere villages, not cities, and none possessed gold or other wealth. One of Coronado's men later wrote, "The villages are somewhat larger than those of Cíbola, and in other respects, in food and everything, they are of the same sort, except that these raise cotton." In addition to growing cotton, the Hopis raised livestock, including sheep, which they herded in the arid region. The American Indians who inhabited these villages, in what is now northeastern Arizona, belonged to the Hopi people.

Don Pedro de Tobar's party encountered the Hopis, a group of American Indians living in what is northeastern Arizona today.

The Hopis

The Hopis were and remain mainly an agricultural people, who grow corn and cotton and raise sheep. Many Hopi artisans still craft jewelry and baskets in the same manner as their ancestors.

A Giant Hole in the Ground

Though Don Pedro and his party returned to report that they had found nothing of importance, they did have one interesting piece of information. The Hopis they had visited had told them that farther to the west lay a great river. Coronado was intrigued. Did this river lead to the sea? If so, it might provide the inhabitants of New Spain with a means of transporting people and goods far inland. Coronado assembled another search party, this one commanded by Don Garcia

Lopez de Cardenas, the officer who had saved his life in the recent battle.

Don Garcia led his group west to Hopi country. From there, a friendly Hopi guided the Spaniards westward for several more days. Finally, they reached the great river that today is called the Colorado. But at first, Don Garcia and his followers were not sure that this river was as large as the American Indians claimed. This was because it was very far

Don Garcia and his party wanted to get to the bottom of the Grand Canyon to reach the Colorado River.

away, at the bottom of a giant hole in the ground. "The sides [of the hole]," one of the Spaniards remarked, "were such a steep rocky precipice [cliff] that it was scarcely possible to see the river, which looks like a brook from above." Don Garcia and his men had become the first Europeans ever to gaze at one of the world's greatest natural wonders—the Grand Canyon!

Don Garcia and his followers searched for a way down into the Grand Canyon, but failed. Pedro de Castañeda wrote this account of their efforts: "They spent three days . . . looking for a passage down to the river, which looked from above as if the water was six feet across, although the Indians said it was half a **league** [about a mile and a half] wide. It was impossible to descend, for [three of the Spaniards] made an attempt to go down . . . . [But] they returned about four o'clock in the afternoon, not having succeeded in reaching the bottom on account of the great difficulties they had found."

California, Texas, and Beyond

Following Coronado's orders, Melchior Diaz took twenty-five men and headed due west in search of the Pacific Ocean. Melchior never reached the Pacific, but he crossed the Colorado River at a point much further south than where it winds through the Grand Canyon. He became the first European to set foot on the soil of what is now California.

Meanwhile, still another party of twenty Spaniards, led by Hernando de Alvarado, struck out toward the east. In

northeastern New Mexico, a region they called Tiguex, they found many villages inhabited by friendly American Indians. And in September 1540, one of the men wrote, "we found a river that runs north and south." This was the Rio Grande, the fifth longest river in North America.

By late autumn 1540, Coronado felt strong enough to lead his own exploratory group. He met up with Alvarado in Tiguex and spent the winter there. Unfortunately, trouble erupted between the Spaniards and the American Indians in the area, and several hundred of the Indians were killed. One

In Tiguex, Hernando de Alvarado found the Rio Grande.

The Most Monstrous Animal?

Alvarado and his men were also the first Europeans to see American bison, sometimes called buffalo. The Spaniards thought that the buffalo was a weird variety of cow. "The most monstrous thing in the way of animals which has ever been seen," is the way one of Alvarado's men described the first one he saw. In those days, untold millions of these beasts roamed the American plains.

of these Indians proved very cooperative, however. Coronado and his men called him "the Turk" because his dark **complexion**, or skin tone, reminded them of people from Turkey. The Turk guided the Spaniards farther eastward, into what is now the narrow strip of Texas known as the Panhandle.

From there, they headed north into Oklahoma and eventually into Kansas, in what is now the American Midwest. Calling the region Quivira, Coronado declared, "The country

itself is the best I have ever seen for producing all the products of Spain, for beside the land [earth] itself being very fat and black and being very well watered by the . . . springs and rivers, I found prunes . . . and nuts and very good sweet grapes and **mulberries**."

What Coronado had *not* found was gold, which had been the expedition's primary goal. By this time, the Spaniards had concluded that the legend of the Seven Cities was just that—a legend! After traveling thousands of miles and exploring huge, previously uncharted territories, Coronado decided that he and his men had had enough of the unknown. Late in 1541, they turned southward toward a more familiar horizon—the one that led to home.

In Quivira, Coronado found rich soil and a wealth of wild fruits.

Coronado's expedition traveled to Tiguex to wait for spring to begin their journey home.

Chapter Five

Return to New Spain

Bidding farewell to the flat, grassy plains of what is now Kansas, Coronado and his men traveled back to Tiguex. Among the native villages they encountered in that largely dry, rocky region were a large group of pueblos lining both sides of the Rio Grande. The Spaniards spent the winter of 1541–1542 in these pueblos, hoping to strike out for home in the spring. As it turned out, Coronado was lucky he made it any further. This is because he suffered a very serious injury while wintering at Tiguex. One day he went out to have a friendly horse race with one of his officers, Don Rodrigo Maldonado. In the middle of the race, a leather strap holding Coronado's saddle suddenly broke. And as Pedro de Castañeda told it in his narrative of the expedition: "He fell over on the side where Don Rodrigo was, and as his horse passed over him it hit his head with its hoof, which laid him at the point of death."

A Cheerless Homecoming

Coronado's recovery was slow and painful. But he steadily improved and managed to get back on his feet in time for the homeward trek, which began in early April 1542. The trip was largely uneventful, and Coronado and his army reached Mexico City in the summer of the same year.

Overall, it proved to be a cheerless homecoming for several reasons. First, by this time Coronado's company was much smaller that it had been when it had departed from Compostela some two and a half years before. Of the original three hundred Spanish soldiers, fewer than a hundred made it back. Of those missing, many had died of injuries or disease on the trip, while the others had deserted. The deserters feared that the authorities in New Spain might punish them for using force to **subdue** some of the Indian villages they had encountered. Many of the American Indian servants and African slaves in the original company did not make it back either. Also absent from the homecoming were some friars

Early Missionaries

When Coronado's expedition returned to New Spain, Father Juan de Padilla and Friar Luis de Ubeda stayed behind as **missionaries**. Father Juan journeyed back to Kansas. There, the native people killed him when he insisted on visiting an enemy tribe. No one knows what happened to Friar Luis.

who had stayed behind to try to convert the native peoples to Christianity.

The viceroy, Mendoza, was naturally concerned that the expedition had sustained such heavy losses. But what bothered him much more was the fact that Coronado had returned empty-handed. The explorers had failed to find any of the gold and other riches that the king and viceroy had hoped they would. Mendoza had spent a great deal of his own money to help finance the expedition, and now he had nothing to show for his **investment**.

Coronado's Sad Final Years

As for Coronado, he too had little to show for all of his time and effort. Like Mendoza, the explorer had sunk much of his own money into the venture. Now almost penniless, Coronado was also out of favor with the viceroy and could expect no more appointments or other favors from him. At least this is what Castañeda's account claims. Some modern historians think that Castañeda may have exaggerated a bit.

What is certain is that Coronado had to make excuses to the king, who had expected so much of him and his expedition. In October 1541, for example, while spending the winter at Tiguex, the explorer had written a letter to Charles V. Fortunately, the letter, in which Coronado admits that he failed to achieve his primary goal, has survived. "I have done all that I possibly could to serve Your Majesty," it begins. But unfortunately, "there were none of the things there of which Friar Marcos had told." Indeed, there were no great cities and no storehouses of treasure. "What I am sure of is that there is not any gold," the letter continues, "nor any other metal in all that country . . . . [There are] nothing but little villages, and in many of these they do not plant anything and do not have any houses except of skins and sticks, and they wander around with the cows [i.e., follow the buffalo]."

Making matters worse, the Spanish authorities in New

A deeply disappointed Coronado wrote the king, telling him of the failure of his expedition.

Spain brought Coronado to trial on charges of mishandling the expedition in 1545. The court ended up finding him not guilty. But his reputation was badly damaged anyway. When Coronado died of illness in Mexico City on September 22, 1554, at the age of forty-four, he was probably a sad man whose passing few Spaniards even noticed.

Coronado's Legacies

In the centuries following Coronado's death, his contributions to the exploration of North America were largely forgotten. Not until the 1940s did modern historians begin to give him the credit he deserves. Seen through modern eyes, Coronado's end is doubly sad. This is because he did not live long enough

Coronado never fully understood the treasures he had found—natural resources, such as Colorado River.

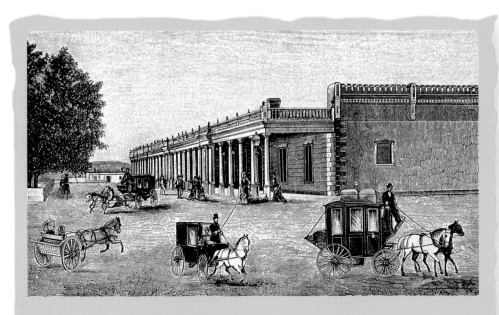

Santa Fe's Blend of Cultures

Built in the early 1600s, the Palace of the Governors was one of the first buildings erected by the Spanish in Santa Fe. Still standing, it is now a museum that displays art and **artifacts** of the region's unique blend of Indian and Spanish cultures.

to find out just how important his discoveries actually were. Indeed, they turned out to be infinitely more valuable than the gold he set out and ultimately failed to find. For example, he and his expedition were the first Europeans to see the Colorado River and the Rio Grande, the Grand Canyon, the plains of Oklahoma and Kansas, and the vast herds of buffalo that roamed the American West. In time, these natural resources proved to be priceless for the descendants of other Europeans who came to the Americas. And eventually, the regions Coronado explored became part of a new and swiftly expanding country—the United States.

Another of Coronado's legacies was his introduction of Spanish culture to the American Southwest. In the late 1500s and on into the 1600s, other Spaniards followed the trails he had blazed and began to settle in the region. In 1609, for example, Pedro de Peralto led a group of **homesteaders** through the region Coronado's party had called Tiguex. There they established Santa Fe, which later became an important city and the capital of the state of New Mexico. Many other towns and sites in the American Southwest still retain Spanish names, customs, and architectural styles.

Back in the 1540s, Coronado could not have foreseen all of these far-reaching developments. All he knew was that he had searched for legendary treasures and had failed to find them. As it happened to other individuals now viewed as great explorers, many years passed before people came to realize the true significance of his efforts. Coronado may have died forgotten by most of his fellow Spaniards and the rest of the world, but today he and his exploits are remembered and recognized by millions of people in many countries.

Timeline

Circa 1000	The roots of the legend of seven Spanish bishops dates back to this era. Supposedly they sailed from Europe to the Americas, where they established seven cities, each filled with gold and other riches.
1492	Italian navigator Christopher Columbus reaches the West Indies, proving that new lands exist on the far side of the Atlantic Ocean.
Circa 1510	Coronado is born in Spain.
1519–1521	Spanish soldier Hernando Cortés conquers the Aztecs and claims Mexico for the Spanish king.
1528	A Spaniard named Pánfilo de Narváez sets out to explore the mysterious lands lying north of Mexico and disappears.
1535	Coronado sails to Mexico, then called New Spain, where he becomes an important local figure.
1537	Coronado marries Beatriz de Estrada, the daughter of a wealthy Spaniard.
1539	The governor of New Spain sends Friar Marcos de Niza to search for the Seven Cities of Gold. On his return, the friar claims that these cities may exist.
1540	The governor appoints Coronado leader of a full-scale expedition, which heads north into Cíbola, the area now occupied by Arizona and New Mexico. Coronado and his men find many Indian villages and discover several large rivers and the Grand Canyon. They also become the first Europeans to see herds of buffalo.
1541	Coronado explores parts of what are now Texas, Oklahoma, and Kansas.
1542	In April, Coronado's expedition heads for home. They reach Mexico City in the summer.
1545	Spanish authorities put Coronado on trial on a charge of mishandling his expedition. He is found not guilty.
1554	Coronado dies of illness in Mexico City.

Glossary

arquebus—a primitive gun developed by the Spanish and French

artifact—a tool, weapon, utensil, sculpture, or other object left behind by a previous culture

cavalry—soldiers mounted on horses

complexion—skin tone

fidelity—loyalty

friar—a priest

homesteader—a pioneer or settler who intends to build a home in an undeveloped region

investment—an outlay of money or other valuables in hopes of making a profit

league—a measurement of distance equal to about 3 miles (5 km)

maize—a kind of corn grown by the Indians of the American Southwest

mass—an important religious service in the Catholic faith

massacre—a large-scale killing

missionary—a person who attempts to convert others to his or her religious beliefs

mulberry—a juicy, dark-purple type of berry

Muslim—a follower of the religion of Islam

pueblo—an American Indian village typical of the American Southwest. The houses are usually made of dried mud and packed close together.

stout—strong, solid

subdue—to overcome, or conquer

viceroy—the governor of a Spanish colony or territory

wayfarer—a traveler

To Find Out More

Books

Jacobs, William J. *Coronado: Dreamer in Golden Armor.* Danbury, CT: Franklin Watts, 1994.

Kent, Deborah. *New Mexico.* Danbury, CT: Children's Press, 1999.

Marcovitz, Hal. *Francisco Coronado and the Exploration of the American Southwest.* Philadelphia: Chelsea House, 2000.

Morris, John Miller. *From Coronado to Escalante: The Explorers of the Spanish Southwest.* Philadelphia: Chelsea House, 1992.

Stein, R. Conrad. *Mexico.* Danbury, CT: Children's Press, 1998.

Stein, R. Conrad. *The World's Great Explorers: Francisco de Coronado*. Chicago: Children's Press, 1992.

Weisberg, Barbara. *Coronado's Golden Quest*. Raintree/Steck-Vaughn, 1992.

Organizations and Online Sites

Coronado National Memorial
4104 East Montezuma Canyon Road
Hereford, AZ 85615-9376
http://www.nps.gov/coro
The Coronado National Memorial was established to honor the first major European exploration of the American Southwest.

The Hopi
http://www.nau.edu/~hcpo-p/
Learn more about the American Indians that Coronado encountered during his expedition.

Map of the Expedition
http://www.lib.utexas.edu/Libs/PCL/Map_collection/National_parks/Coronado_Expedition.jpg
A colorful, useful map showing the routes followed by Coronado and members of his expedition from 1540 to 1542.

The West

http://www.pbs.org/weta/thewest/wpages/wpgs400/w4corona.htm

The companion site for the PBS documentary *The West* features a summary of Coronado's adventures and some useful links to related topics.

A Note on Sources

In writing this book about Coronado, I first consulted the primary, or original, sources, which is the standard procedure that historians follow. Primary sources are most often old letters, journals, poems, inventory lists, legal documents, and religious and other inscriptions carved into stone or some other durable material; as well as chronicles written by ancient and other pre-modern historians. Such sources are not always as informative and reliable as we would like them to be. But they provide at least a partial picture of long-dead societies as drawn by the members of those societies. In the case of Coronado's expedition, the primary sources consist of a number of chronicles written by members of Coronado's company, as well as two surviving letters penned by the explorer himself.

By contrast, modern books and articles written about bygone eras and cultures are known as secondary sources. They typically attempt to weave together a coherent narrative based on the primary sources and to speculate about the nature of any events and information on which the original documents shed no light. This book about Coronado, for instance, is a secondary source. Of the more scholarly secondary sources I used in writing it, Stewart Udall's book about Coronado's life and exploits, *Majestic Journey: Coronado's Inland Empire*, was particularly well written and helpful.

—*Don Nardo*

Index

Numbers in *italics* indicate illustrations.

About the Author

Don Nardo is a historian and award-winning writer. Among his many books about the history of North America are *The North American Indian Wars*, a comprehensive summary of the European conquest of the American Indian tribes in what is now the United States; *The Mexican-American War*, which exposes the complex background, dirty politics, and needless brutality of one of America's forgotten conflicts; *Braving the New World*, the inspiring saga of the first black slaves in colonial America; and *The Declaration of Independence*, a detailed overview of the history and legacy of that famous document. He also wrote *France* for the Enchantment of the World series. Mr. Nardo lives with his wife Christine in Massachusetts.